WITTY & FRIENDS
REAL ESTATE
ACTIVITY & COLORING BOOK

OPEN HOUSE

FOR SALE

WITTY REALTY

Welcome!

Hey kids! This book was created to help make your move a little easier. Your realtor is here to help your family find your new home. They also help you sell your home. Realtors are friendly and want the best for you and your family.

You may see construction workers, appraisers, mortgage brokers and movers around your home. They are helping your family with your move.

When you box up your favorite books, toys and clothes, you'll see them again in your new home. Try to remember to be helpful and have a great attitude while you are making the transition.

In this book, you'll learn more about moving, how to make new friends, and how to be helpful during your move.

My favorite realtor is: _____

Contact number: _____

E-mail address: _____

Website: _____

PLACE YOUR
BUSINESS CARD
HERE

WITTY & FRIENDS, MY PALS.

Witty is my pal.
He is out of sight.
We dance and sing to our favorite songs.
March 1, 2, 3. Right, left, right.

Foxy is my buddy.
He packs up his favorite toy.
We love our realtor who helps us
find a cool place to live.
When he gets to his new home, he'll find it with joy.

Brainy is my friend.

He will help load up the car to help his family out.

Treat others the same and be kind.

There is no need to cry or pout.

Buzzy stays busy doing activities inside and out.
He is helpful and nice to all.
He loves to make honey and it tastes so sweet.
Buzzy, your new neighbor,
might ask you if you want to play ball.

Nutty is a funny squirrel.
She reads bedtime stories to me and my friends.
She tells jokes and laughs with us.
Kindness helps us win.

Gritty is super cool.
He flies high and spreads his wings.
He has a heart of gold.
Gritty loves to dance and sing.

When they go to sleep, they have sweet dreams.
Witty & Friends are so kind.
They make me laugh.
Happy memories are always on my mind.

Witty & Friends rock!

They are champions for a great cause.

My buddies, my friends, my pals.

We will give them our loudest applause.

Witty & Friends are smart.
They love to read.
They need help with this activity book.
Will you help them, please?

COLOR YOUR DREAM HOUSE.

REAL ESTATE TERMS

- **AGENT** – A PERSON AUTHORIZED TO ACT FOR AND UNDER THE DIRECTION OF ANOTHER PERSON WHEN DEALING WITH THIRD PARTIES.

- **CLOSING** – THE CONCLUSION OF THE SALES TRANSACTION WHEN THE SELLER TRANSFERS TITLE TO THE BUYER IN EXCHANGE FOR CONSIDERATION.

- **CONTRACT** – A LEGALLY ENFORCEABLE AGREEMENT TO DO, OR NOT TO DO, A PARTICULAR THING FOR A CONSIDERATION.

- **DEED** – A WRITTEN INSTRUMENT BY WHICH TITLE TO LAND IS CONVEYED.

- **DEPRECIATION** – A LOSS IN VALUE.

- **EQUITY** – THE DIFFERENCE IN DOLLARS BETWEEN A HOUSE'S VALUE AND THE MORTGAGE AMOUNT.

- **LANDLORD** – THE OWNER OF ANY REAL ESTATE, SUCH AS A HOUSE, APARTMENT BUILDING OR LAND, THAT IS LEASED OR RENTED TO ANOTHER PERSON, CALLED THE TENANT.

- **OPEN HOUSE** – AN OPPORTUNITY FOR PROSPECTIVE BUYERS TO VIEW A HOUSE IN A LOW PRESSURE ENVIRONMENT.

- **PRINCIPAL** – THE AMOUNT OF MONEY OWED TO THE LENDER NOT INCLUDING INTEREST.

- **REAL ESTATE** – REFERS TO LAND AND IMPROVEMENTS AND THE RIGHTS TO OWN OR USE THEM.

- **REAL ESTATE AGENT** – A PERSON LICENSED TO NEGOTIATE AND TRANSACT THE SALE OF REAL ESTATE ON BEHALF OF THE PROPERTY OWNER.

- **REAL ESTATE APPRAISER** – A PERSON LICENSED TO LEGALLY APPRAISE REAL ESTATE PROPERTY FOR A FEE.

- **REAL ESTATE BROKER** – A PERSON LICENSED TO LEGALLY REPRESENT A PURCHASER OF REAL ESTATE PROPERTY FOR A FEE.

- **TITLE** – THE RIGHT OF OWNERSHIP OF A PROPERTY.

- **UNDERWRITING** – THE PROCESS OF VERIFYING DATA AND APPROVING A LOAN.

WoRD SCRaMBLERS

CSOLNGI

1. _____

EDED

2. _____

NCRATOTC

3. _____

YQUETI

4. _____

RAEL EESTTA

5. _____

ANOLDLRD

6. _____

LIAPRCPNI

7. _____

NGTEA

8. _____

ITELT

9. _____

WORD SEARCH

```
P J F D H L P F Z L R R T R X
R U N T E O I L A E E E N Y C
G A R A N N U S E Y A K E I Q
L N S C A O I S Z H L O M T V
V E I N H A I N E F T R T T M
M F C W R A H T M I O B S V A
L E U P O M S W C W R H E B R
E Q P N G H N E D E E D V O S
R A C R E D S Y E U P G N X W
M O N E Y Q X B B G N S I E A
S D N E I R F F B I O T N S L
M O R T G A G E V O W J Q I B
Q L S F L F D O H B N J C N J
W U K C M N M N B A W U Q H H
I W I G J J J G K K Y V F S A R
```

HELP BRAINY FIND THESE WORDS

ACRE	APPRAISAL	BOXES
BROKER	DEED	FINANCE
FRIENDS	FUN	HELP
HOUSE	INSPECTION	INVESTMENT
LAND	LAWS	LEASE
MONEY	MORTGAGE	MOVING
OWN	PURCHASE	REALTOR
	SHOWING	

WHAT DO YOU WANT YOUR NEW BEDROOM TO LOOK LIKE?
DESIGN IT WITH BEDDING, CURTAINS, FURNITURE, TOYS,
BOOKS, GAMES, AND MORE! BE CREATIVE.

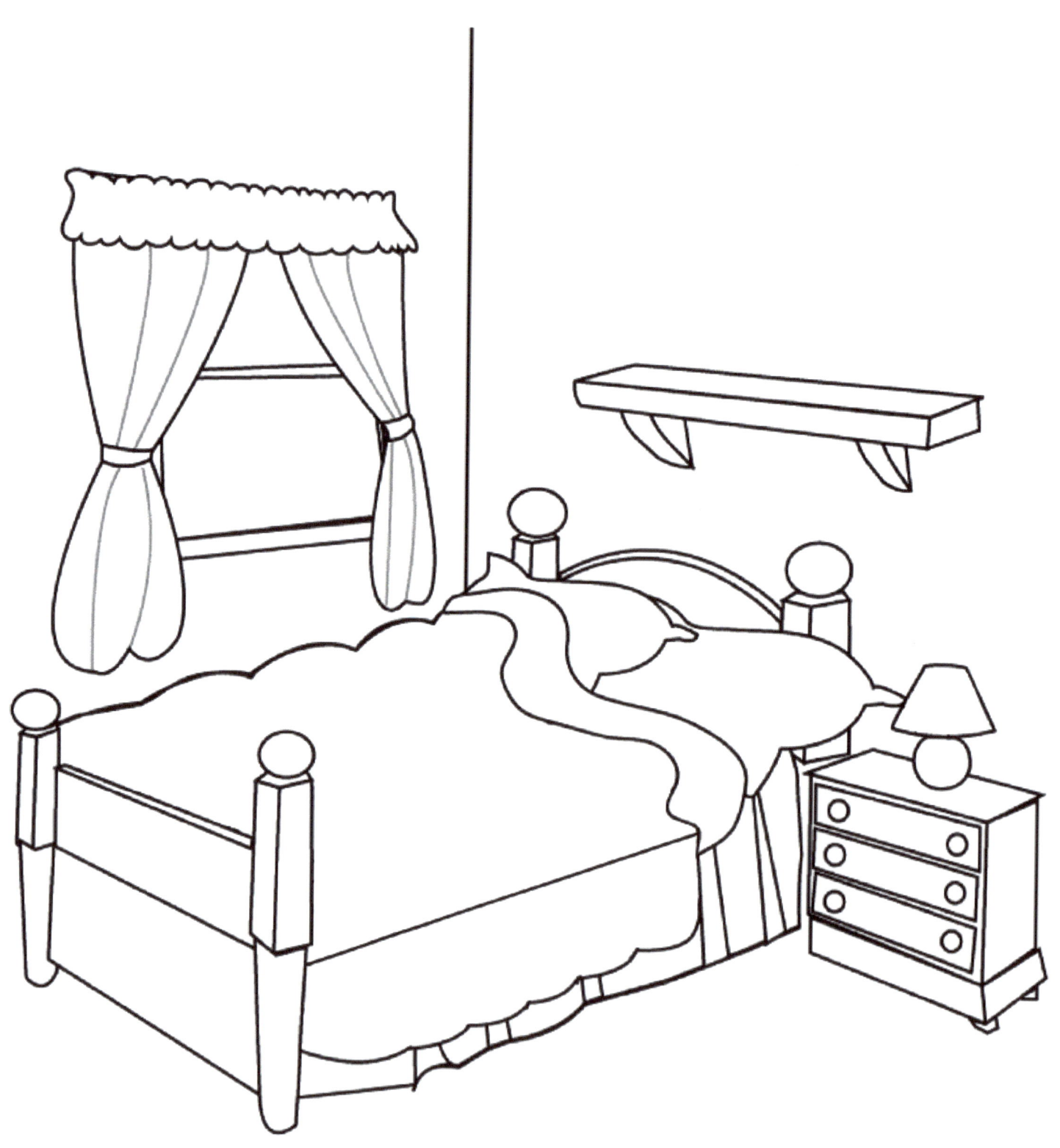

CAN YOU FIND YOUR WAY TO YOUR NEW HOUSE?

START

FINISH

MOVING TO A NEW PLACE CAN BE FUN.

How do you make new friends?

1) Ask your parents to help you meet new kids in the neighborhood. Always be safe.

2) Be kind. Say nice words and try to be helpful.

3) Ask your new friends about their favorite books, toys, vacations, movies, and more.

4) Be brave. Don't be afraid to talk to new kids.

5) Smile. Sometimes, a smile helps others know that you are a nice person.

YOUR REAL ESTATE AGENT WILL HELP YOU FIND JUST THE RIGHT HOUSE FOR YOUR FAMILY. THEY ARE HERE TO HELP YOU.

DRAW YOUR NEW HOUSE USING THESE SHAPES.

CIRCLE

SQUARE

TRIANGLE

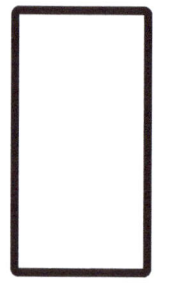

RECTANGLE

RHOMBUS

PACK YOUR THINGS INSIDE THIS MOVING BOX. DON'T WORRY. IT WILL BE WAITING FOR YOU AT YOUR NEW HOUSE.

CONNECT THE DOTS
TO CREATE A HOUSE.

CAN YOU FIND 5 DIFFERENCES IN THESE PICTURES?

MY MOVING IN/OUT ✔ CHECKLIST

Bedrooms

_____
_____
_____
_____
_____
_____

Kitchen

_____
_____
_____
_____
_____
_____

Living Room

_____
_____
_____
_____
_____

Garage

_____
_____
_____
_____
_____

Darla Hall has a heart for helping others. This activity book concept was developed in 2012 when a young boy she knew was hit by a car and broke both of his legs. He is fully recovered and she continues her mission to help more kids through donations of her books. Her company, Witty Publications, now has over 35 titles. Hall resides in Indiana and has three sons. She loves to help others throw their own touchdowns in business and in life through her motivational speaking. Please follow Darla Hall and Witty Publications on Facebook & Instagram.

Thank you for your support.

QB Darla Hall

Created by Author QB Darla Hall
Follow us on social media!